GRAPHIC DINOSAURS

VELOCIRAPTOR

THE SPEEDY THIEF

ILLUSTRATED BY JAMES FIELD

Rosen Classroom Books & Materials ™
New York

Published in 2008 by The Rosen Publishing Group, Inc.
29 East 21st Street, New York, NY 10010

Designed and produced by
David West Books

Designed and written by David West
Editor: Gail Bushnell
Consultant: Steve Parker, Senior Scientific Fellow, Zoological Society of London
Photographic credits: 5t, Ty Smith; 5bl, Helen Jobson; 5br, Bob Ainsworth;
31, Fighting Dinosaur Fossil: © American Museum of Natural History.

Library of Congress Cataloging-in-Publication Data

West, David.
Velociraptor : the speedy thief / David West.
p. cm. — (Graphic dinosaurs)
Includes index.
ISBN-13: 978-1-4042-3898-5 (library binding) ISBN-10: 1-4042-3898-0 (library binding)
ISBN-13: 978-1-4042-9628-2 (pbk.) ISBN-10: 1-4042-9628-X (pbk.)
ISBN-13: 978-1-4042-9670-1 (6 pack) ISBN-10: 1-4042-9670-0 (6 pack)
1. Velociraptor—Juvenile literature. 2. Dinosaurs—Juvenile literature. I. Title.
QE862.S3W47 2008
567.912—dc22

2007008673

Manufactured in China

CONTENTS

WHAT IS A VELOCIRAPTOR?

VELOCIRAPTOR MEANS "SPEEDY THIEF"

◀ *A long, stiff tail helped it balance.*

◀ *Velociraptor had forward-facing eyes so it could judge distances when hunting* **prey.**

It had long jaws with about 80 sharp, curved teeth.

It had large hands with sharp claws for gripping its prey.

➡ *Some of its skin was probably coated in feathers to keep it warm.*

➡ *Powerful legs meant it could reach speeds of 40 mph (64 km/h).*

➡ *It had a large, sharp claw on each foot. This was raised off the ground when it ran, to keep the claw from getting blunt.*

VELOCIRAPTOR LIVED AROUND 85 TO 75 MILLION YEARS AGO, DURING THE **CRETACEOUS** PERIOD. **FOSSILS** OF ITS SKELETON HAVE BEEN FOUND IN MONGOLIA, RUSSIA, AND CHINA (SEE PAGE 30).

Adult Velociraptors measured up to 5.9 feet (1.8 m) long, 2 feet (0.62 m) high at the hip. They weighed 45 pounds (20 kg) or perhaps twice this amount.

FEATHERED DINOSAURS

Fossils of **ancestors** of Velociraptor show that they had feathers. Some scientists think that it was coated in feathers to keep it warm, like feathers in a padded jacket or comforter.

HOOKED CLAW

This fossil of Velociraptor's claw is 3.5 inches (9 cm) long. It has a sharp point but does not have a sharp blade. Velociraptor used the claws like hooks, to hang on to its prey while it attacked with its teeth. The teeth had **serrated** edges, like steak knives, so they could bite through skin and muscle more easily.

Dinosaur and bird fossils sometimes show evidence of feathers, like this Archaeopteryx.

PACK HUNTERS

Velociraptor probably lived and hunted in packs, like **African wild dogs** do today.

MODERN ANCESTORS

The skeleton of Velociraptor is similar to the kiwi, a flightless bird living in New Zealand today. Experts think Velociraptor might have been warm-blooded like modern birds.

PART ONE... THE INVADER

MONGOLIA. 75 MILLION YEARS AGO. THE CRETACEOUS PERIOD.

A PACK OF VELOCIRAPTORS IS NESTING IN A FOREST ON THE EDGE OF A DESERT.

HIDDEN IN THE FOREST, A FEMALE VELOCIRAPTOR GUARDS HER EGGS.

SHE PROTECTS THEM FROM OTHER ANIMALS THAT MIGHT WANT TO EAT THEM, EVEN HER OWN KIND.

SHE SEES A SMALL LIZARD. SHE HAS NOT EATEN FOR 24 HOURS, BUT SHE DOES NOT DARE LEAVE HER EGGS ALONE.

HISSSSSSS

SOME VELOCIRAPTORS ARE RETURNING FROM A HUNTING TRIP.

THEY HAVE NOT BEEN SUCCESSFUL. HUNGER MAKES THEM ILL TEMPERED.

ANOTHER FEMALE HAS LEFT HER NEST UNGUARDED AND A HUNGRY MALE STEALS ONE OF HER EGGS.

THERE IS A SCUFFLE AS OTHERS JOIN IN TO FIGHT FOR THE FOOD.

THE VELOCIRAPTORS SUDDENLY STOP FIGHTING.

THEY FEEL A FAINT SHUDDER THROUGH THE GROUND...

...AND ANOTHER. THE VELOCIRAPTORS HIDE.

ABOVE THEIR HEADS, GIANT CLAWS RIP AT THE BRANCHES. IT IS A THERIZINOSAURUS, A GIANT PLANT-EATING DINOSAUR.

CRACK

ALTHOUGH IT IS NOT A THREAT TO THE VELOCIRAPTORS, IT IS STEADILY HEADING IN THE DIRECTION OF THE NESTING AREA.

THE VELOCIRAPTORS TRY TO DISTRACT THE THERIZINOSAURUS.

THE THERIZINOSAURUS LOOKS DOWN ON THE VELOCIRAPTORS AND SLOWLY SWINGS ITS GIANT CLAWS AT THEM.

THE CLAWS SHAKE A SMALL MAMMAL, ZALAMBDALESTES, FROM A TREE.

TWO VELOCIRAPTORS FIGHT OVER THE FALLEN MAMMAL.

SWISHHHH

GIANT CLAWS CATCH THE TWO FIGHTING VELOCIRAPTORS AND KNOCK THEM OUT.

THE VELOCIRAPTORS CONTINUE TO DISTRACT THE THERIZINOSAURUS AND EVENTUALLY IT TURNS BACK.

THE TIRED VELOCIRAPTORS RETURN TO THE NESTING SITE.

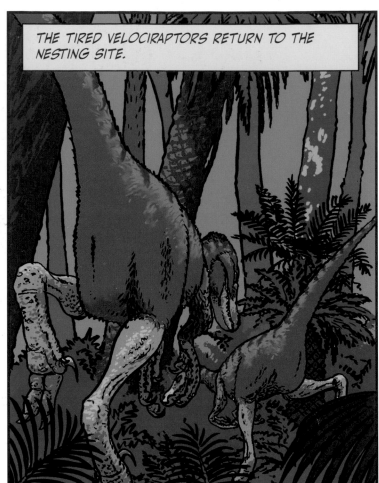

A MOTHER HEARS HER **HATCHLINGS** CALLING FROM THEIR EGGS...

KEEK KEEK

...THE EGGS BEGIN TO CRACK...

CRICK

...EVENTUALLY, TWO MALES ARE FREE FROM THEIR EGGS. THEY ARE THE FIRST OF SEVERAL VELOCIRAPTORS TO HATCH OVER THE NEXT FEW DAYS.

KEEK

OVER THE FOLLOWING WEEKS THE HATCHLINGS STAY CLOSE TO THE NESTING SITE.

HERE THEY PRACTICE HUNTING. THEY CAPTURE INSECTS, LIZARDS, AND SMALL MAMMALS.

THE TWO BROTHERS LEARN THAT THEY CATCH MORE IF THEY HUNT TOGETHER.

THEY LEARN THAT SOME THINGS ARE NOT SO GOOD TO EAT...

...AND SOME THINGS ARE GOOD TO EAT, BUT DIFFICULT TO CATCH.

THEY ALSO LEARN TO HIDE FROM DANGER BY DARTING UNDER COVER. EVEN THE ADULTS MIGHT EAT THEM.

PART TWO

SURVIVAL

THE BROTHERS ARE NOW OLD ENOUGH TO HUNT ON THEIR OWN. THEY HAVE SEEN A GROUP OF MONONYKUS HATCHLINGS.

THEY MUST BE CAREFUL. THEY MOVE FORWARD SLOWLY. IF THEY GET TOO CLOSE THE MONONYKUS WILL SEE THEM AND ESCAPE.

THE USUALLY ALERT MONONYKUS DO NOT KNOW THEY ARE BEING WATCHED.

SUDDENLY, THE VELOCIRAPTORS BURST FROM THE UNDERGROWTH. THE MONONYKUS ARE TAKEN BY SURPRISE.

THE BROTHERS HONE IN ON THE SLOWEST.

THE STRUGGLE IS SHORT. THE VELOCIRAPTORS ARE SUCCESSFUL.

KRAAR

THEY HAVE NO TIME TO ENJOY THEIR MEAL, THOUGH. A HUNGRY ADULT VELOCIRAPTOR HAS DISCOVERED THEM.

GRAAR

THE BROTHERS MUST LOOK ELSEWHERE FOR FOOD.

THE NEXT DAY, SEVERAL YOUNG VELOCIRAPTORS FIND A HERD OF GALLIMIMUS FEEDING ON A SWARM OF DRAGONFLIES.

THEY JOIN IN THE FEEDING FRENZY.

THE ADULTS HIDE IN THE SHADOWS, WATCHING FOR A WEAK OR OLD GALLIMIMUS THEY CAN PREY ON.

SUDDENLY, AN ALIORAMUS CHARGES OUT FROM HIDING.

GRAARRR

THE GALLIMIMUS SEE THE ALIORAMUS AND SOUND A WARNING AS THEY RUN AWAY.

HONK

THE HERD SCATTERS. THE YOUNG VELOCIRAPTORS HAVE TO RUN FOR THEIR LIVES.

HONK

SOME MAKE IT TO THE SAFETY OF THE FOREST. OTHERS ARE NOT SO LUCKY.

HONK

A GALLIMIMUS HAS FALLEN AND BROKEN ITS NECK. THE ADULT VELOCIRAPTORS FIND IT AND FEED ON THE DEAD BODY.

THE YOUNGSTERS PATIENTLY WAIT FOR THEIR TURN, FROM A SAFE DISTANCE. HUNGRY VELOCIRAPTORS ARE DANGEROUS, EVEN TO THEIR OWN KIND.

ROAR

BUT THE ALIORAMUS HAS SMELLED THE BLOOD AND RETURNS TO FIND THE DEAD GALLIMIMUS.

THE VELOCIRAPTORS KNOW THEY ARE NO MATCH FOR THIS FIERCE MEAT-EATER AND RUN AWAY.

THE BROTHERS RETURN TO THE SITE OF THE SWARM OF DRAGONFLIES.

HERE, THEY SPOT BIRDS FEEDING ON THE CRUSHED BODY OF A VELOCIRAPTOR.

CAREFULLY, THEY STALK THE BIRDS.

ONE OF THEM ATTACKS THE BIRDS, WHICH SCATTER INTO THE AIR TO ESCAPE FROM HIM. THE SECOND BROTHER LEAPS FROM A ROCK AND CAPTURES ONE OF THE BIRDS IN THE AIR.

THE MEAL IS EATEN IN SECONDS, FEATHERS AND ALL.

PART THREE... RIVALS

THE VELOCIRAPTOR PACK IS OUT HUNTING. THE YOUNGSTERS ARE NEARLY FULL-GROWN. THEY HAVE LOST THEIR JUVENILE MARKINGS AND THEIR ADULT FEATHERS ARE SHOWING.

THE BROTHERS HAVE SPOTTED AN OLD BACTROSAURUS BUT HAVE BECOME SEPARATED FROM THE REST OF THEIR PACK.

SKREEK SKREEK

THEY CALL OUT TO THE PACK.

THE REPLY THEY HEAR DOES NOT SOUND FAMILIAR.

SKRAAK

SKRAA

SKRAA

SUDDENLY, A STRANGE GROUP OF VELOCIRAPTORS APPEARS.

EVEN THOUGH THEY'RE AFRAID, THE BROTHERS STAND THEIR GROUND.

HISSSS

HISSSS

THE STRANGERS BEGIN TO MOVE FORWARD. THEY WANT TO KILL THE BROTHERS.

THE REST OF THE PACK ARRIVES JUST IN TIME.

THE STRANGERS TURN TO FACE THE NEW THREAT.

THE TWO PACKS FACE EACH OTHER, DECIDING WHAT TO DO NEXT.

THE STRANGERS ARE OUTNUMBERED...

...AND DECIDE TO RETREAT INTO THE FOREST.

ONE OF THE BROTHERS REMEMBERS THE BACTROSAURUS AND CALLS TO THE PACK.

SKREK SKREK

THE PACK FOLLOWS THE BROTHERS TO A RIDGE.

LOOKING DOWN FROM THE RIDGE, THEY SEE THE OLD BACTROSAURUS WALKING ACROSS THE PLAIN.

THE PACK RACES DOWN THE SLOPE TO CATCH THE OLD BACTROSAURUS.

THEY LEAP ONTO HIS BACK AND NECK, CLINGING WITH THEIR SHARP-CLAWED HANDS AND THE **RETRACTABLE** CLAW ON THEIR HIND LEGS. THEN THEY BITE WITH THEIR RAZOR-SHARP TEETH.

DRAARGH

THE BACTROSAURUS IS TOO OLD AND WEAK TO PUT UP A FIGHT. HE SOON DIES FROM LOSS OF BLOOD.

THE PACK EATS QUICKLY. THERE ARE PLENTY OF LARGER PREDATORS WHO COULD EASILY STEAL THEIR MEAL.

AN OVIRAPTOR LOOKS ON. IT KEEPS A SAFE DISTANCE. THE OVIRAPTOR IS NO MATCH AGAINST A PACK OF VELOCIRAPTORS.

THE VELOCIRAPTORS LEAVE. A TYRANNOSAURUS BATAAR SMELLS THE CARCASS AND COMES TO FEED ON THE LEFTOVERS.

PART FOUR... THE STORM

THE BROTHERS ARE OUT HUNTING WITH THE PACK AGAIN, IN THE DESERT. A CLAP OF THUNDER PROMISES MUCH-NEEDED RAIN.

CRACK

RUMBLE

RUMBLE

FROM A DRY GULLY ON THE EDGE OF THE DESERT, THE TWO BROTHERS WATCH A PROTOCERATOPS' NESTING SITE.

A SMALL MONITOR LIZARD TRIES TO STEAL AN EGG...

...BUT THE MOTHER CHASES IT AWAY.

THE LIZARD RUNS PAST THE TWO BROTHERS, BUT THEY IGNORE IT. THEY ARE MORE INTERESTED IN A PROTOCERATOPS AT THE EDGE OF THE NESTING SITE.

THE APPROACHING STORM IS MAKING THE PROTOCERATOPS NERVOUS.

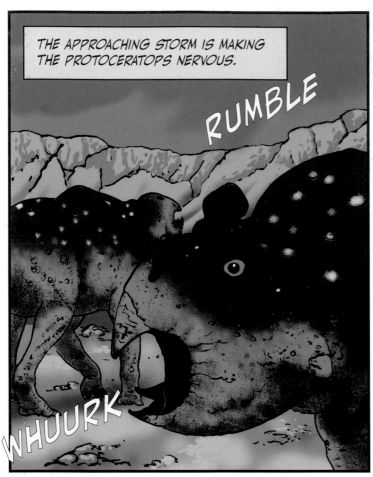

AS THE BROTHERS WATCH, THE REST OF THE VELOCIRAPTOR PACK CREEP AROUND TO THE OTHER SIDE OF THE NESTING SITE.

THE SKIES OPEN AND RAIN POURS DOWN. THE BROTHERS ATTACK. THE REST OF THE PACK WAIT IN AMBUSH.

THE PROTOCERATOPS RUN IN ALL DIRECTIONS.

WHAARK

WHAARK

WHAARK

VISIBILITY IS POOR AND THE BROTHERS LOSE SIGHT OF EACH OTHER AND THEIR PREY.

CRACK

ONE OF THE BROTHERS PASSES A NEST FULL OF EGGS AND FORGETS ABOUT THE HUNT.

CRUNCH

SLURP

THE NOISE OF THE STORM STOPS THE VELOCIRAPTOR FROM HEARING THE RETURNING PROTOCERATOPS MOTHER.

SHE CHARGES AND CATCHES THE BROTHER IN THE CHEST.

HAARGH

HE TURNS AND GRABS HER, SINKING HIS CLAWS INTO HER NECK.

SKREEEK

WHAARK

ABOVE THEM, THE RAIN HAS MADE THE SANDBANK UNSAFE.

CREEK

SKREEEK

WHAARK

SUDDENLY, THE BANK COLLAPSES. THEY ARE BOTH KILLED INSTANTLY.

WHUMP!

THE SURVIVING BROTHER AND THE REST OF THE PACK HAVE KILLED A PROTOCERATOPS AND ARE FEEDING ON IT IN THE RAIN.

THE SURVIVING BROTHER LOOKS UP. HE REALIZES HIS BROTHER IS MISSING, BUT HUNGER KEEPS HIM FEEDING.

THE PACK HEADS OFF TO DIGEST THE MEAL IN SAFETY. THEY STOP BY THE GULLY, WHICH IS NOW FLOODED. THE SURVIVING BROTHER WATCHES A HERD OF PRENOCEPHALE IN THE DISTANCE, FEEDING ON SHRUBS. FOR THE TIME BEING, HE DOES NOT FEEL HUNGRY. THE RAIN HAS STOPPED AND THE SUN IS WARM ON HIS BACK. AT LAST HE CAN REST FOR A WHILE.

FOSSIL EVIDENCE

WE HAVE A GOOD IDEA OF WHAT DINOSAURS MAY HAVE LOOKED LIKE FROM STUDYING THEIR FOSSIL REMAINS. FOSSILS ARE FORMED WHEN THE HARD PARTS OF AN ANIMAL OR PLANT BECOME BURIED AND THEN TURN TO ROCK OVER MILLIONS OF YEARS.

One of the most amazing dinosaur fossils ever found was dug up in 1971 in Mongolia. It shows a fight between a Protoceratops and a Velociraptor. The Protoceratops bites the Velociraptor's arm as the Velociraptor strikes back at its throat with the claw on its left leg.

For the dinosaurs to be caught in this pose, scientists believe they died instantly. A collapsing sand dune is one likely reason. A large amount of wet sand falling on the two dinosaurs would set like concrete and preserve their pose, as seen today (below).

DINOSAUR GALLERY

ALL THESE DINOSAURS APPEAR IN THE STORY.

Mononykus
"Single claw"
Length: 3 ft (1 m)
A small, birdlike dinosaur with a single claw on each stubby arm.

Protoceratops
"First horned face"
Length: 7 ft (2 m)
A medium sized plant-eater with a large armored neck frill.

Oviraptor
"Egg thief"
Length: 6 ft (1.8 m)
A birdlike dinosaur with a parrotlike beaked mouth.

Prenocephale
"Sloping head"
Length: 8 ft (2.5 m)
A small, dome-headed plant-eater.

Gallimimus
"Chicken Rooster mimic"
Length: 20 ft (6 m)
A large, ostrichlike dinosaur with a beaklike mouth.

Bactrosaurus
"Club-spined lizard"
Length: 20 ft (6 m)
A plant-eater of the duck-billed dinosaur or hadrosaur type.

Tyrannosaurus bataar
"Tyrant lizard of bataar"
Length: 40 ft (13 m)
A large meat-eater, weighing 5 tons (4,550 kg).

Alioramus
"Different branch"
Length: 20 ft (6 m)
A smallish tyrannosaur, weighing 1 ton (910 kg).

Therizinosaurus
"Scythe lizard"
Length: 39 ft (12 m)
A giant plant-eater with long finger claws.

GLOSSARY

African wild dogs (A-frih-kun WY-uld DOGZ) Wild dogs that live in packs on the African grasslands. Their main prey is impala, a type of buck.

ancestor (AN-ses-ter) Earlier animal from which a later animal evolved.

Cretaceous period (krih-TAY-shus PIR-ee-ud) The time between 146 million and 65 million years ago.

fossils (FAH-sulz) The remains of living things that have turned to rock.

hatchlings (HACH-lingz) Young animals that have hatched from eggs.

prey (PRAY) Animals that are hunted for food by another animal.

retractable (ree-TRAK-ta-bull) Something that can be drawn back.

serrated (ser-AYT-ed) Having a jagged toothed edge, like a saw.

INDEX

Web Sites

Due to the changing nature of Internet links, the Rosen Publishing Group, Inc., has developed an online list of Web sites related to the subject of this book. This site is updated regularly. Please use this link to access the list:

www.powerkidslinks.com/gdino/vrap/